WORLD'S GREATEST

# DAD JOKES

## 160

**HILARIOUS KNEE-SLAPPERS AND HOKEY PUNS**

T0076887

13-Digit ISBN: 978-1-60433-879-9

10-Digit ISBN: 1-60433-879-2

This book may be ordered by mail from the publisher. Please include $5.99 for
postage and handling. Please support your local bookseller first!

Books published by Cider Mill Press Book Publishers are available at special
discounts for bulk purchases in the United States by corporations, institutions,
and other organizations. For more information, please contact the publisher.

Cider Mill Press Book Publishers
"Where good books are ready for press"
501 Nelson Place
Nashville, Tennessee 37214
Visit us online!
cidermillpress.com

Typography: Adobe Garamond, BodoniFB, Clarendon,
Futura, Hanley Sans, Helvetica, Industry Inc.

Printed in Malaysia
23 24 25 26 27 COS 11 10 9

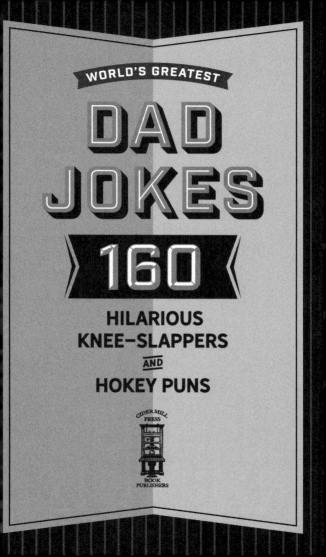

**WORLD'S GREATEST**

# DAD JOKES

## 160

### HILARIOUS KNEE-SLAPPERS

**AND**

### HOKEY PUNS

CIDER MILL PRESS

BOOK PUBLISHERS

# Contents

# Did You Hear the One About the Dad Jokes?

We call them "Dad Jokes," but anyone can tell them. Moms tell them to kids, aunts and uncles tell them to the family, and friends tell them to other friends. But we call them "Dad Jokes" because they're best delivered by a Dad.

Dads are traditionally the goof-balls, the clowns of the family; unafraid to embarrass themselves in the on-going quest to entertain their children and themselves. That's a Dad thing. Dads scare the neighborhood kids on Halloween. Dads put too many lights on the house during the holidays. Dads buy fireworks. Dads will throw you in the pool. Dads will make an ass of themselves just to get a laugh.

Sure, Moms are funny! But Moms are the responsible ones; the ones who make sure we mind our manners. A Mom will never ask you to pull her finger. But a Dad will…

And that's why we call them Dad Jokes. So, what exactly defines these jokes?

Dad Jokes have a few things in common: they have to be short, they have to be simple, and they have to be fairly clean. A Dad Joke is one that can entertain most any kid of any age.

A Dad may tell a dirty joke, but a dirty joke is not a Dad Joke. A Dad may tell a long rambling joke with a great punchline, but that's not a Dad Joke. Physical humor, gross-out jokes, parodies — not Dad Jokes.

Most Dad Jokes are bad puns or simple one-liners. Some of them are smart-aleck replies. Still others verge on the absurd. Almost all of them are embarrassingly corny. And that's the key to a good Dad Joke — the embarrassment! Dad Jokes are best told to children in front of their best friends, causing eye-rolls, exasperation, and the sudden urge to disappear. The best Dad Jokes illicit groans, followed by a brief snicker, and then a sustained smile. Job done.

And what about knock-knock jokes? Are they Dad Jokes? We think not. Some of the first jokes kids tell are knock-knock jokes, the currency of grade-school humor. And while knock-knock jokes are funny, their universality and predictability disqualify them as Dad Jokes.

The greatest Dad Jokes utilize the element of surprise. You just don't see it coming! Dad will slip the set-up line into everyday conversation, and then — BAM! — a punchline that you should have seen coming, but now can't escape. And in these modern times, Dad Jokes are ready-made for texting, transcending the bounds of distance and time. These days, no child is safe.

But forewarned is forearmed: what follows are dozens and dozens of the best Dad Jokes around. If you're a Dad (or a Mom, or just a lover of silly jokes), here's an arsenal of groaners for all occasions, ready to be sprung upon unsuspecting victims when the time is just right.

And if you're the son or daughter of a wiseacre Dad, here's your chance to turn the tables and get even. You'll be ready for whatever Dad delivers. As Noah said while filling the ark, "Now I herd them all!"

# 1.

## DID YOU HEAR . . . ?

# Did you hear the joke about paper?

It's tear-able.

# Did you hear about the restaurant on the Moon?

Great food, but no atmosphere.

# Did you hear about the man who was buried alive?

**It was a grave mistake.**

# Did you hear
# about the two radios
# that got married?

THE RECEPTION WAS FANTASTIC.

..................................................................

# Did you hear
# about the new
# corduroy pillows?

THEY'RE MAKING HEADLINES.

# Did you hear about the new automatic shovel?

It's a groundbreaking invention.

# Did you hear about the fire in the shoe factory?

**Hundreds of soles were lost.**

**Did you hear
about the thieves
who fell in wet cement?**

THEY WERE HARDENED CRIMINALS.

**Did you hear
about the population
of Ireland?**

IT'S DUBLIN.

# DID YOU HEAR ABOUT THE TWO THIEVES WHO STOLE A CALENDAR?

*They each got six months.*

# DID YOU HEAR ABOUT THE SAD WEDDING CAKE?

It was in tiers.

# Did you hear about the fire at the campground?

It was in tents!

# DID YOU HEAR ABOUT THE NEW JANITORS' UNION?

*It's sweeping the nation.*

# DID YOU HEAR ABOUT THE BAGUETTE AT THE ZOO?

It was bread in captivity.

# Did you hear about the clown who held doors for people?

It was a nice jester.

# Did you hear about the butcher who backed into the meat grinder?

HE GOT A LITTLE BEHIND IN HIS WORK.

# Did you hear about the runner who got teased?

HE TOOK IT ALL IN STRIDE.

# Did you hear about the guy who killed a man with sandpaper?

He only wanted to rough him up.

# Did you hear about the cow who jumped over barbed wire?

It was udder destruction.

# DID YOU HEAR ABOUT THE GUY WHO INVENTED TIC TACS?

They say he made a mint.

# Did you hear about the claustrophobic astronaut?

He just needed space.

**Did you hear about
the computer that got
the Miley Virus?**

IT STOPPED TWERKING.

**Did you hear about the
tongue-twister champion
who got arrested?**

HE GOT A REALLY TOUGH SENTENCE.

# Did you hear about the semicolon who got arrested?

HE GOT TWO CONSECUTIVE SENTENCES.

# Did you hear about the invisible man who married the invisible woman?

THE KIDS WERE NOTHING TO LOOK AT.

# Did you hear about the rock that was 1,760 yards long?

**It must be a milestone!**

# Did you hear the cyclops closed his school?

**He only had one pupil.**

# 2.

# HOW MANY . . . ?

# HOW MANY TICKLES DOES IT TAKE TO MAKE AN OCTOPUS LAUGH?

*Ten-tickles.*

# HOW MANY PEOPLE DOES IT TAKE TO CHANGE A LIGHT BULB IN MEXICO?

Just Juan.

# How much does a pirate pay for corn?

## A buccaneer.

# How do you catch
# a unique rabbit?

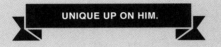

**UNIQUE UP ON HIM.**

...........................................................

# How do you catch
# a tame rabbit?

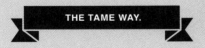

**THE TAME WAY.**

# HOW LONG DOES A JOUSTING MATCH LAST?

Until knight fall.

# HOW DOES A YETI BUILD HIS HOUSE?

Igloos it together.

# How do you catch a squirrel?

Climb a tree and act nuts.

# How do you make a Swiss roll?

Push him down the mountain.

# How do you fix a broken tuba?

With a tuba glue.

# How do you know there's an elephant in your refrigerator?

You can't shut the door.

# HOW DOES A TRAIN EAT?

It goes chew chew.

# How does Darth Vader know what Luke got him for Christmas?

He felt his presents.

# How do prisoners call each other?

Cell phones.

# HOW DID THE EGYPTIANS SELECT THE NEXT PHARAOH?

*It was a pyramid scheme.*

**3.**

**WHY . . . ?**

# WHY CAN'T YOU HAVE A NOSE 12 INCHES LONG?

Because then it would be a foot.

# Why can't you hear a pterodactyl go to the bathroom?

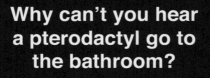

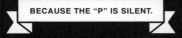

BECAUSE THE "P" IS SILENT.

# Why can't humans hear a dog whistle?

BECAUSE DOGS CAN'T WHISTLE.

# Why can't blind people go skydiving?

**Because it scares the hell out of the dogs!**

# Why couldn't the lifeguard rescue the hippie?

He was too far out.

# Why don't they play poker in Africa?

Too many cheetahs.

# Why don't cannibals eat clowns?

Because they taste funny.

# Why don't melons get married?

They cantaloupe.

# Why don't skeletons like scary movies?

They don't have the guts.

# Why don't oysters share their pearls?

They're shellfish.

# Why don't you tell pigs secrets?

THEY MAY SQUEAL.

............................................................

# Why don't you ever see hippos hiding in trees?

BECAUSE THEY'RE REALLY GOOD AT IT.

# Why shouldn't you write with a broken pencil?

**BECAUSE IT'S POINTLESS.**

# Why shouldn't you buy Velcro?

**IT'S A RIPOFF.**

# Why is 6 afraid of 7?

Because 7 8 9.

# Why are there walls around graveyards?

Because people are dying to get in.

# WHY ARE THERE FEWER FROGS THAN BEFORE?

*Because they keep croaking.*

# Why are horse-drawn carriages so unpopular?

Because horses are bad at drawing.

# Why was the math book in therapy?

Because it had so many problems.

# WHY DO COWS WEAR BELLS?

Because their horns don't work.

# WHY DO COWS MOO?

Because farmers have cold hands.

# Why do gorillas have big nostrils?

BECAUSE THEY HAVE BIG FINGERS.

# Why do bees hum?

BECAUSE THEY DON'T KNOW THE WORDS.

# Why do bananas wear sunscreen?

**Because they peel easily.**

# Why does Moon rock taste better than Earth rock?

**Because it's meteor.**

# Why does our solar system get such bad ratings?

**Because it only has one star.**

# Why do trees seem so suspicious?

Because they're a bit shady.

# Why did the scarecrow win an award?

He was outstanding in his field.

# Why did the bicycle fall over?

It was two-tired.

# Why did the golfer change his pants?

Because he got a hole in one.

# Why did the pony drink some tea?

He was a little horse.

# Why did the turkey cross the road?

To prove he wasn't chicken.

# Why did the boy get a new butt?

His old one was cracked.

# Why did the shopping cart quit its job?

It was tired of being pushed around.

# WHY DID THE SCIENTIST REMOVE HIS DOORBELL?

He wanted to win the no-bell prize.

# Why did the old man fall in the well?

BECAUSE HE COULDN'T SEE THAT WELL.

---

# Why did the man quit railroad engineer school?

HE COULDN'T STAY ON TRACK.

# Why did the police officer stink?

Because he was on duty.

# Why did Humpty Dumpty have a great fall?

Because his summer was miserable.

# Why did the cowboy adopt a dachshund?

He wanted to get a long little doggy.

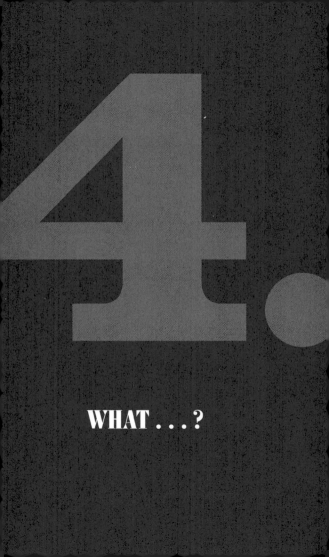

# 4.

## WHAT . . . ?

# What did the Buddhist say to the hot dog vendor?

Make me one with everything.

# What do lawyers wear to court?

Lawsuits.

# WHAT DO YOU DO WITH EPILEPTIC LETTUCE?

Make a seizure salad.

# What do yetis get from sitting on the ice too long?

POLAROIDS.

# What do snowmen do in their spare time?

THEY'RE JUST CHILLIN'.

**WHAT DO YOU SAY TO A HITCHHIKER WITH ONE LEG?**

*Hop in!*

# What do you do with an elephant with 3 balls?

Walk him and pitch to the giraffe.

# What does Charles Dickens keep in his spice rack?

The best of thymes, the worst of thymes.

# What side of a duck has the most feathers?

The outside.

# What kind of bees make milk?

Boo-bees.

# What's a zebra?

26 sizes larger than an "A" bra.

# What's the best way to carve wood?

Whittle by whittle.

# What's the best thing about living in Switzerland?

I dunno, but the flag is a big plus.

# WHAT KIND OF TEACHER NEVER FARTS IN PUBLIC?

A private tutor.

# WHAT'S THE DUMBEST ANIMAL IN THE JUNGLE?

A polar bear.

# What's Irish and stays out all night?

**Patty O'Furniture.**

# What has four wheels and flies?

**A garbage truck.**

# WHAT WASHES UP ON TINY BEACHES?

Microwaves.

# What has four legs and can fly?

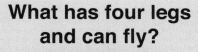

TWO BIRDS.

.................................................

# What's the best time to go to the dentist?

TOO-TH HURTY.

# WHAT HAPPENS WHEN YOU GET HIT WITH A RENTAL CAR?

*It Hertz.*

# What state has the smallest soft drinks?

Minnesota.

# What happens when you watch a ship wreck?

You let it sink in.

# What did the fish say when he ran into the wall?

Dam!

# What did the buffalo say when his son left for school?

**Bison.**

**What did the duck say when he bought lip balm?**

PUT IT ON MY BILL.

**What did the monkey say when he caught his tail in the door?**

IT WON'T BE LONG NOW.

# WHAT DO PORCUPINES SAY WHEN THEY KISS?

Ouch.

# What did the pirate say when he turned 80?

Aye, matey!

# What did Cinderella say when her photos didn't arrive?

Someday my prints will come.

**What did George Washington say to his troops before crossing the Delaware?**

GET IN THE BOAT.

. . . . . . . . . . . . . . . . . . . . . . . . . . . . . . . . . . . . . . . . . . . . . . . . . . . . . . . . . . . . . . . .

**What goes "Oh, oh, oh"?**

SANTA WALKING BACKWARD.

# What's the difference between a hippo and a Zippo?

ONE'S A LITTLE LIGHTER.

.........................................................

# What's the difference between roast beef and pea soup?

ANYONE CAN ROAST BEEF.

# What's the difference between an African elephant and an Indian elephant?

About 5,000 miles.

# What's the difference between ignorance and apathy?

I don't know, and I don't care.

# WHAT'S THE DIFFERENCE BETWEEN A SNOWMAN AND A SNOWWOMAN?

*Snowballs.*

# What do you get when you cross a cow and a shark?

I don't know, but I wouldn't want to milk it.

# What's the difference between beer nuts and deer nuts?

Beer nuts are 49 cents,
deer nuts are just under a buck.

# What's the difference between an oral thermometer and a rectal thermometer?

The taste.

# What do you get when you cross an elephant with a rhino?

Ell-if-I-know.

# What do you get when you cross a four-leaf clover with poison ivy?

**A rash of good luck.**

# What do Alexander the Great and Winnie the Pooh have in common?

Their middle name.

# What do you call a hippie's wife?

Mississippi.

# What do you get when you cross an insomniac, an agnostic, and a dyslexic?

Someone who stays up all night wondering if there really is a dog.

# WHAT DO YOU CALL CHEESE THAT ISN'T YOURS?

Nacho cheese.

# WHAT DO YOU CALL A LADY WITH ONE LEG?

Eileen.

# What do you call a bullfighter with a rubber toe?

**Roberto.**

# What do you call a Frenchman walking on the beach?

**Phillipe Flop.**

# What do you call a cow that ate a stick of dynamite?

ABOMINABLE.

. . . . . . . . . . . . . . . . . . . . . . . . . . . . . . . . . . . . . . . . . . . . . . . . . . . .

# What do you call that cow when it explodes?

NOBLE.

# What do you call a man who tames lions?

CLAUDE.

...............................................................

# What do you call a dog with no legs?

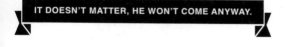

IT DOESN'T MATTER, HE WON'T COME ANYWAY.

# What was the
# hot dog's name?

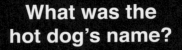

FRANK.

# Who married a
# hamburger?

PATTY.

# WHAT'S RED AND MOVES UP AND DOWN?

A tomato in an elevator.

# What's red and smells like blue paint?

Red paint.

# What's red and bad for your teeth?

**A brick.**

# What's brown and sticky?

A stick.

# What's black and red and black and red and black and red?

**A zebra with a sunburn.**

# What's small, red, and whispers?

**A hoarse radish.**

# WHAT'S BROWN AND SOUNDS LIKE A BELL?

Dung.

# WHAT'S WHITE AND CAN'T CLIMB A TREE?

A refrigerator.

# 5.

ME & DAD

**ME:**
Dad, did you get your haircut?

**DAD:**
I got them all cut!

---

**ME:**
Dad, I'm hungry.

**DAD:**
Hi, Hungry, I'm Dad!

**ME:**
Dad, is today
Wednesday?

**DAD:**
All day!

---

**ME:**
Dad, it's cold in here.

**DAD:**
Go stand in the
corner where it's
90 degrees.

**ME:**
Dad, what time is it?

**DAD:**
Time to get a new watch!

---

**ME:**
How do I look?

**DAD:**
With your eyes!

**ME:**
Dad, can you put
my shoes on?

**DAD:**
I don't think they'll
fit me!

---

**ME:**
Dad, what's on TV?

**DAD:**
Dust.

**ME:**
Dad, can you make me a sandwich?

**DAD:**
Abracadabra—
you're a sandwich!

---

**ME:**
Dad, are you all right?

**DAD:**
No, I'm all left!

**ME:**
Dad, can you put
the cat out?

**DAD:**
I didn't know he
was on fire!

---

**ME:**
Dad, can I watch TV?

**DAD:**
Sure, just don't
turn it on.

**ME:**
Dad, I'm gonna
take a shower.

**DAD:**
Well, you'd better
put it back!

━━━━━━━━━━━━━━━━━━━

**ME:**
Dad, where are
my sunglasses?

**DAD:**
I don't know, where
are my dad glasses?

**ME:**

Dad, I'll call you later.

**DAD:**

Please, just call me Dad.

### About Cider Mill Press Book Publishers

Good ideas ripen with time. From seed to harvest, Cider Mill
Press brings fine reading, information, and entertainment
together between the covers of its creatively crafted books.
Our Cider Mill bears fruit twice a year, publishing
a new crop of titles each spring and fall.

"Where Good Books Are Ready for Press"

Visit us online at
cidermillpress.com
or write to us at
501 Nelson Place
Nashville, Tennessee 37214